now you're cookin'

SMOOTHIES

Colophon

Original recipes and photos: © R&R Publishing Pty. Ltd.

Design and layout: AdAm Studio, Prague, The Czech Republic

Cover design: Minkowsky Graphics, Enkhuizen, The Netherlands

Proofreading: Sarah Dunham

ISBN 13: 978-90-366-2103-8

now you're cookin'

SMOOTHIES

THIS BOOK JUST MAKES YOU WANNA COOK -

REBO PUBLISHERS

Introduction

Fruit blended with other healthy ingredients into a smooth, tasty beverage–that's a smoothie. Smoothies are quick and easy to make–you can take one with you on the go. With a blender and this collection of recipes, you'll soon be mixing and drinking all sorts of tantalizing concoctions and getting the vitamins and nutrients you need to boot!

PRINCESS
P 0 I II

Serves **2**

Method

Place all ingredients in blender; blend until SMOOTH!

Pour into chilled glass and serve topped with a sprinking of muesli.

Mango Morning Smoothie

Ingredients

1/2 cup milk

Flesh of 1/2 mango

1/4 banana

1/2 cup plain yogurt

1 teaspoon toasted muesli

1 tablespoon date paste

3 ice cubes

Serves **2**

Method

Place all ingredients in blender; blend until SMOOTH!

Pour into chilled glass and serve topped with a sprinkle of nutmeg.

Banana Smoothie

Ingredients

1/2 cup milk

1 1/2 banana

1/2 cup plain yogurt

1 teaspoon honey

2-3 drops vanilla essence

a dash of nutmeg

4 ice cubes

Serves **2**

Method

Place all ingredients in blender; blend until SMOOTH!

Pour into chilled glass and serve topped with half a fresh strawberry.

Strawberry Smoothie

Ingredients

1/2 cup milk

6 frozen strawberries

1/2 cup plain yogurt

1 teaspoon honey

2-3 drops vanilla essence

a pinch of nutmeg

4 ice cubes

Serves **2**

Method

Place all ingredients in blender; blend until SMOOTH!

Pour into chilled glass and serve topped with a fresh strawberry, a few blueberries and a dusting of vanilla sugar.

Banana Berry Smoothie

Ingredients

1/2 cup milk

1 banana

6 frozen strawberries

10-12 blueberries

1 teaspoon honey

2 drops of vanilla essence

4 ice cubes

Serves **2**

Method

Place all ingredients in blender; blend until SMOOTH!

Pour into chilled glass and serve with a slice of orange.

Banana Zing Smoothie

Ingredients

1/2 cup milk

1/2 banana

juice of 1 orange

3-4 drops lemon juice

1/2 cup plain yogurt

2 teaspoons apple juice concentrate

4 ice cubes

Serves **2**

Method

Place all ingredients in blender; blend until SMOOTH!

Pour into chilled glass and serve topped with half a strawberry and a swirl of syrup.

Chocolate Berry Smoothie

Ingredients

1/2 cup milk

4 frozen strawberries

8-10 blueberries

1/2 cup plain yogurt

1 tablespoon chocolate syrup

2-3 drops vanilla essence

3 ice cubes

Serves **2**

To serve

Pour into chilled glass and serve topped with a cherry and a swirl of chocolate sauce.

Cherry Smoothie

Ingredients

10 frozen cherries, pitted

1/2 cup plain yogurt

2 teaspoons dark chocolate sauce

2 ice cubes

Place all ingredients in blender; blend until SMOOTH!

Pour in 1/2 cup of coconut milk and stir.

Serves **2**

Method

Place all ingredients in blender; blend until SMOOTH!

Pour in 1/2 cup of coconut milk and stir.

Pour into chilled glass and serve topped with strawberries.

Tropical Frootz Smoothie

Ingredients

1/2 cup milk

1/2 banana

2 strawberries

chunks of pineapple (approx 1/2 cup)

1/2 cup plain yogurt

1 teaspoon honey

2 ice cubes

Serves **2**

Method

Place all ingredients in blender; blend until SMOOTH!

Pour into chilled glass and serve with a swirl of passion fruit pulp.

Passion Frootz

Ingredients

1/2 cup milk

1/2 apple peeled and cut into small

pieces

1/2 banana

juice of one orange

flesh of 1 passion fruit

1/2 cup plain yogurt

1 teaspoon honey

smoothies

Serves **2**

Method

Place all ingredients in blender; blend until SMOOTH!

Pour into chilled glass and serve topped with nutmeg.

Banana Chocolate Nut Smoothie

Ingredients

1/2 cup milk

1 banana

2 tablespoons chocolate sauce

2 tablespoons hazelnut paste

1/2 cup plain yogurt

1 teaspoon honey

2-3 drops vanilla essence

4 ice cubes

Serves **2**

Method

Place all ingredients in blender; blend until SMOOTH!

Pour into chilled glass and serve topped with chocolate buttons.

Banana and Cherry Split Smoothie

Ingredients

1/2 cup milk

1 banana

6 cherries, pitted

1 tablespoon strawberry jam

1 tablespoon chocolate syrup

1/2 cup plain yogurt

2-3 drops vanilla essence

4 ice cubes

smoothies

Serves **2**

Method

Place all ingredients in blender; blend until SMOOTH!

Pour in 1/4 cup of coconut milk and stir.

Pour into chilled glass and sprinkle with toasted coconut.

Lemon Meringue Smoothie

Ingredients

1/4 cup milk

1/2 banana

2 tablespoons lemon butter

1 teaspoon caramel sauce

1/2 cup plain yogurt

2-3 drops vanilla essence

4 ice cubes

Serves **2**

Method

Place all ingredients in blender; blend until SMOOTH!

Pour into chilled glass and serve with colored sprinkles.

Toffee Apple Smoothie

Ingredients

1/2 cup milk

1/2 apple peeled, cored and sliced into small pieces

1 teaspoon apple juice concentrate

4 cherries, pitted

1/2 cup plain yogurt

1 teaspoon toffee flavored syrup

1 teaspoon caramel flavored syrup

2-3 drops vanilla essence

4 ice cubes

Serves **2**

Method

Place all ingredients in blender; blend until SMOOTH!

Pour into chilled glass and serve with a dollop of peanut butter.

Peanut Butter and Jelly Smoothie

Ingredients

1/2 cup milk

1/2 banana

4 strawberries

4 tablespoons peanut butter

1/2 cup plain yogurt

1 teaspoon strawberry jam

4 ice cubes

Serves **2**

Method

Place all ingredients in blender; blend until SMOOTH!

Pour into chilled glass and serve.

Tropical Burst Smoothie

Ingredients

1/4 cup milk

1 kiwi fruit peeled and quartered

3 strawberries

approx 1/2 cup of watermelon, seeded

1/2 cup plain yogurt

1 teaspoon honey

2 ice cubes

Serves **2**

Method

Place all ingredients in blender; blend until SMOOTH!

Pour into chilled glass and sprinkle with cinnamon sugar.

Apple Cherry Pie Smoothie

Ingredients

1/2 cup milk

2 strawberries

3 cherries, pitted

1/2 apple peeled, cored and cut into small pieces

1/2 teaspoon apple juice concentrate

1/2 cup plain yogurt

1 teaspoon caramel syrup

a dash of nutmeg

a dash of cinnamon

2 drops of vanilla essence

3 ice cubes

smoothies

Serves **2**

Method

Place all ingredients in blender; blend until SMOOTH!

Pour into chilled glass and serve topped with toasted coconut.

Strawberry Short Cake Smoothie

Ingredients

1/2 cup milk

6-8 strawberries

1/2 cup plain yogurt

1 teaspoon toffee flavored syrup

1 teaspoon caramel flavored syrup

2 drops vanilla essence

4 ice cubes

a dash of nutmeg

a dash of cinnamon

smoothies

Serves **2**

Method

Place all ingredients in blender; blend until SMOOTH!

Serve in a chilled glass and serve with biscotti and an extra dollop of yogurt and a drizzle of honey.

Pear Danish Smoothie

Ingredients

1/2 cup milk

1/2 cup stewed or roasted pear, chilled

1/2 cup plain yogurt

1/4 cup cream cheese

1/2 teaspoon pear juice concentrate

1/2 teaspoon toffee flavored syrup

2-3 drops vanilla essence

4 ice cubes

A dash of nutmeg

Serves **2**

Method

Place all ingredients in blender; blend until SMOOTH!

Pour into chilled glass and serve topped with berries.

Cherry Fruit Cake Smoothie

Ingredients

1/2 cup milk

1/4 apple peeled, cored and cut into small pieces

4 blueberries

2 cherries, pitted

1/2 banana

1/2 cup plain yogurt

1/2 teaspoon caramel sauce

1/2 teaspoon toffee flavored sauce

1 tablespoon date spread

2 drops vanilla essence

3 ice cubes

A dash of nutmeg

smoothies

Serves **2**

Method

Place all ingredients in blender; blend until SMOOTH!

Pour into chilled glass and serve with ladyfingers.

Tiramisu Smoothie

Ingredients

1/2 cup milk

1/2 teaspoon decaffeinated instant coffee granules

1 banana

1 ladyfinger, crushed

1/2 cup plain yogurt

1/2 teaspoon chocolate sauce

2-3 drops vanilla essence

4 ice cubes

Serves **2**

Method

Place all ingredients in blender; blend until SMOOTH!

Pour into chilled glass and serve topped with toasted coconut.

Apple Crumble Smoothie

Ingredients

1/2 cup milk

1/2 apple (peeled, cored and sliced)

1/2 banana

1/2 cup plain yogurt

1 teaspoon caramel sauce

1/4 cup toasted muesli

2 drops vanilla essence

3 ice cubes

A pinch of cinnamon and nutmeg

smoothies

Serves **2**

Method

Place all ingredients in blender; blend until SMOOTH!

Pour into chilled glass and serve topped with colored sprinkles.

Hawaiian Delight Smoothie

Ingredients

1/2 cup milk

6 cherries, pitted

1/2 cup pineapple chunks

1/2 tangerine

1/2 cup plain yogurt

1 teaspoon honey

2-3 drops vanilla essence

2 ice cubes

Serves **2**

Method

Place all ingredients in blender; blend until SMOOTH!

Pour into chilled glass and serve topped with chocolate shavings.

Jaffa Smoothie

Ingredients

1/4 cup milk

1/2 banana

juice of one orange

1/2 cup plain yogurt

2 teaspoon chocolate syrup

2-3 drops vanilla essence

2 ice cubes

smoothies

Serves **2**

Method

Place all ingredients in blender; blend until SMOOTH!

Pour into chilled glass and serve topped with toasted coconut.

Banana Pudding Smoothie

Ingredients

1/2 cup milk

1 banana

1/2 cup plain yogurt

1/2 teaspoon caramel sauce

1/2 teaspoon toffee sauce

2-3 drops vanilla essence

4 ice cubes

A pinch of nutmeg

Serves **2**

Method

Place all ingredients in blender; blend until SMOOTH!

Pour into chilled glass and sprinkle with cinnamon.

Key Lime Pie Smoothie

Ingredients

1/2 cup milk

1 kiwi fruit, peeled

2 tablespoons lemon butter

1/2 cup plain yogurt

1 teaspoon lime juice

1 teaspoon caramel sauce

2-3 drops vanilla essence

3 ice cubes

A pinch of nutmeg

A pinch of cinnamon

Serves **2**

Method

Place all ingredients in blender; blend until SMOOTH!

Pour into chilled glass and serve topped with blueberries.

Banana Berry Muffin Smoothie

Ingredients

1/2 cup milk

1/2 banana

12 blueberries

1/2 cup plain yogurt

2 teaspoons toffee sauce

1 teaspoon ground almond paste

2-3 drops vanilla essence

4 ice cubes

A pinch of cinnamon and nutmeg

smoothies

Serves **2**

Method

Place all ingredients in blender; blend until SMOOTH!

Pour into chilled glass and serve.

Banapple Smoothie

Ingredients

1/2 cup milk

1/2 banana

half an apple, peeled and cut into

small pieces

1/2 cup plain yogurt

1 teaspoon honey

2-3 drops vanilla essence

3 ice cubes

Serves **2**

Method

Place all ingredients in blender; blend until SMOOTH!

Pour into chilled glass and serve topped with a fanned strawberry.

Tropicana Smoothie

Ingredients

1/2 cup milk

1/2 mango, peeled and sliced

1/2 banana

1/2 apple, peeled and sliced

2 strawberries

1/4 cup plain yogurt

1 teaspoon honey

3 ice cubes

Serves **2**

Method

Place all ingredients in blender; blend until SMOOTH!

Pour into chilled glass and serve topped with passion fruit.

Tropical Zing Smoothie

Ingredients

1/3 cup milk

1/2 an orange

1/4 of a mango, peeled and sliced

pulp of 2 passion fruit

1/2 cup pineapple

1/2 cup plain yogurt

1 teaspoon honey

2 ice cubes

smoothies

Serves **2**

Method

Place all ingredients in blender; blend until SMOOTH!

Pour into chilled glass and garnish with a swirl of passion fruit.

Calypso Smoothie

Ingredients

1/2 cup milk

1/3 cup pineapple

pulp of 2 passion fruit

1/2 banana

1/2 cup plain yogurt

1 teaspoon honey

4 ice cubes

Serves **2**

Method

Place all ingredients in blender; blend until SMOOTH!

Pour into chilled glass and serve.

Fruit Salad Smoothie

Ingredients

1/2 cup milk

1/3 cup of pineapple

2 strawberries

1/3 banana

1/3 apple peeled and cut into small pieces

1/2 cup plain yogurt

1 teaspoon honey

4 ice cubes

Serves **2**

Method

Place all ingredients in blender; blend until SMOOTH!

Pour into chilled glass and serve topped with yogurt and colored sprinkles.

Chocolate Mint Berry Smoothie

Ingredients

1/2 cup milk

1/2 banana

3 strawberries

1 teaspoon chocolate mint sauce

1/2 cup plain yogurt

1 teaspoon strawberry jam

4 ice cubes

smoothies

Serves **2**

Method

Place all ingredients in blender; blend until SMOOTH!

Pour into chilled glass and serve topped with a swirl of caramel syrup.

Cheesecake Smoothie

Ingredients

1/2 cup milk

1/2 cup custard apple (cherimoya) flesh

1/4 cup cream cheese

1/4 cup plain yogurt

1 teaspoon caramel sauce

1 teaspoon hazelnut butter

2 drops vanilla essence

4 ice cubes

A dash of nutmeg

Serves **2**

Method

Place all ingredients in blender; blend until SMOOTH!

Pour into chilled glass and serve topped with a dash of nutmeg.

Custard Apple Smoothie

Ingredients

1/2 cup milk

1/2 cup custard apple (cherimoya) flesh

1/2 banana

1/2 cup plain yogurt

1 teaspoon honey

2 drops vanilla essence

4 ice cubes

Serves **2**

Method

Place all ingredients in blender; blend until SMOOTH!

Pour into chilled glass and serve topped with a dollop of honey.

Honey Smack Smoothie

Ingredients

1/2 cup milk

1/2 cup custard apple (cherimoya) flesh

3/4 cup full of frosted mini-wheats

1/4 cup plain yogurt

2 tablespoons honey

2-3 drops vanilla essence

2 ice cubes

Serves **2**

Method

Place all ingredients in blender; blend until SMOOTH!

Pour into chilled glass and serve topped with muesli.

Muesli Bar Smoothie

Ingredients

1/2 cup milk

1/2 banana

2 tablespoon muesli

1 teaspoon of date pulp

1/2 cup plain yogurt

1/2 teaspoon molasses

2-3 drops vanilla essence

3 ice cubes

Serves **2**

Method

Place all ingredients in blender; blend until SMOOTH!

Pour into chilled glass and serve topped with a sprinkling of cinnamon.

Mango & Orange Smoothie

Ingredients

1/2 cup milk

pulp of 1 mango

juice of 1 orange

1/2 cup plain yogurt

1 teaspoon honey

2 ice cubes

Serves **2**

Method

Place all ingredients in blender; blend until SMOOTH!

Pour into chilled glass and serve topped with half an Oreo or chocolate biscuit.

Banario Smoothie

Ingredients

1/2 cup milk

1 banana

2 Oreo cookies, crushed

1/3 cup plain yogurt

4 ice cubes

smoothies

Serves **2**

Method

Place all ingredients in blender; blend until SMOOTH!

Pour into chilled glass and serve topped with a dollop of yogurt and a sprinkling of toasted coconut

Pear and Coconut Delight Smoothie

Ingredients

1/2 cup milk

1/2 cup stewed or roasted pear, chilled

1/2 cup plain yogurt

1 teaspoon honey

2 tablespoons of toasted coconut

1 teaspoon pear concentrate

2 drops vanilla essence

4 ice cubes

Serves **2**

Method

Place all ingredients in blender; blend until SMOOTH!

Pour into chilled glass and serve sprinkled with a crushed malt biscuit.

Monte Carlo Smoothie

Ingredients

1/2 cup milk

1/2 apple peeled, cored and sliced

1/2 banana

1 teaspoon macadamia paste

1/2 cup plain yogurt

1 teaspoon raspberry jam

2-3 drops vanilla essence

A pinch of nutmeg

2 ice cubes

Serves **2**

Method

Place all ingredients in blender; blend until SMOOTH!

Pour into chilled glass and serve topped with extra muesli.

Anzac Cookie Smoothie

Ingredients

1/2 cup milk

1/2 cup plain yogurt

1/2 cup stewed or roasted pear, chilled

1/2 cup toasted muesli

2 teaspoons golden syrup

3 drops of vanilla essence

3 ice cubes

smoothies

Serves **2**

Method

Place all ingredients in blender; blend until SMOOTH!

Pour into chilled glass and serve topped with toasted coconut.

Iced Vovo Smoothie

Ingredients

1/2 cup milk

1/4 cup coconut milk

1/2 apple peeled, cored and sliced

2 strawberries

1/2 cup plain yogurt

1 teaspoon raspberry jam

1 teaspoon macadamia paste

2 drops vanilla essence

2 ice cubes

Serves **2**

Method

Place all ingredients in blender; blend until SMOOTH!

Pour into chilled glass and serve topped with an extra dollop of yogurt and some passion fruit pulp.

Sunrise Surprise Smoothie

Ingredients

1 blood orange peeled and seeded

the pulp of half a mango

the pulp of 2 passion fruit

1/2 cup plain yogurt

1 teaspoon honey

2–3 drops vanilla essence

4 ice cubes

smoothies

Serves **2**

Method

Place all ingredients in blender; blend until SMOOTH!

Pour into chilled glass and serve topped with cinnamon.

Apricot Danish Smoothie

Ingredients

1/4 cup milk

1/2 cup stewed or roasted apricots, chilled

1/4 cup plain yogurt

1/4 cup cream cheese

1/4 cup apricot nectar

1/2 teaspoon honey

2-3 drops vanilla essence

4 ice cubes

A dash of nutmeg and cinnamon

Serves **2**

Method

Place all ingredients in blender; blend until SMOOTH!

Pour into chilled glass and serve topped with chunks of frozen melon.

Melon Mix Smoothie

Ingredients

1/4 cup milk

1/3 banana

1/2 cup watermelon flesh, seeded

1/2 cup honeydew or cantaloupe flesh

1/2 cup plain yogurt

1 teaspoon honey

2-3 drops vanilla essence

3 ice cubes

smoothies

Index